WIV 10/17

This boo[k]   [fro]m's way
so that we ha[ve]   [a]s we should.

Please return this book on or before
the date shown above.
To renew go to **libraries.essex.gov.uk/** or ring
0345 603 7628 or go to any Essex library.

Essex County Council

Foreword by the author:

Most of the anecdotes within this book were told to me first hand, and I have endeavoured to relate them as accurately as possible. These stories are by no means unique - they are similar to the stories of our past being told all over this country. All you have to do is listen.

Any profits from the sale of this book, made by The Royal Norfolk Regiment D-Day Veteran's Association, will be donated to charity and/or used for upkeep of memorials. Thank you for your donation.
If you did not buy this book, next time Remembrance Sunday comes around, please dig deep.

We will remember them all.

J. R. Jones.

Introduction

The Royal Norfolk Regiment 1st Battalion D-Day Veterans Association was formed in 1979, and has endured for many decades. The Association has included all ranks, and veterans who have served in all theatres of war, not just D-Day. But most importantly for the group: it has included family and friends in it's ranks. Many books have been written about World War Two; most of them tell stories of the great leaders and the grand armies they led, clashing in mighty battles to decide the fate of the world. This one is different. This one is more about the individual, and the effect such a cataclysmic event a World War has on their family and friends. These stories and photos follow the veterans, their families and friends, in war, in peace, and in remembrance. This book is heavy with photographs, and each one tells a story in it's own right. Some are in black and white, some are in colour. All of them show images of moments frozen in time. For everyone you see in the photos, they capture a small moment of their life; the smell of the soil as they trudge across a field; the weather beating down as they smile at the camera; a shared joke with friends; being covered in dust from a convoy of military vehicles leaving a newly liberated town; a sombre moment stood at the graveside of a friend. All aspects of a journey that took many people away from their homes into the maelstrom of war. Those who survived have repeated that journey many times, to pay their respects to those who fell. Men stand by gravestones with their families and friends. They point to someone they knew as a young man, who never had the chance to be with their families again, and there is always a sense of tragic loss. Yet at the same time there is an overwhelming feeling of support - a brotherhood for want of a better word - for as long as one person remembers, be they veteran, family or friend, the loss somehow becomes an easier burden to carry.

Happy Birthday!

As we walk along I am amazed at what I have just been told:

"So let me get this straight." I ask. "You were nineteen on D-Day? The 6th June is your birthday?"

The old man smiles at me, the ends of his grey moustache twitch with delight.

"Yes – the 6th June 1944 – I was nineteen to the day as I came off that landing craft." He drops his voice as we walk along. "Don't tell everyone though – it gets very tiring having to listen to every French reception committee singing 'Happy Birthday'!"

Naively I stammer out the first thing that comes into my head:

"Did you get any birthday presents on D-Day?"

He stops and looks at me as if wondering if I have had a bit too much sun.

"No, no birthday presents."

We continue our walk in silence, then he leans conspiratorially into my shoulder:

"Got a bit of shrapnel though."

Sword Beach, June 2004.

Above and Below: Sword Beach, 1944.

Above: Beach and defences, 2004.

Right: Moving inland from Sword Beach, 1944.

On Sword Beach

A mixed group of us stand near the beach. Old soldiers, family and friends, talking about the weather and what we were likely to have for tea later that day. The conversation meanders along as only it can amongst friends. One old soldier talks about his training on how to fight in the close quarters of a house:

"In England." He says. "They set up an entire complex of varying heights to train for it. One person threw in a charge, the next went in with a Sten to clear the room. The rest followed in behind. Easy enough – but you had to do it fast, no hanging about. Bang! Goes the charge – in you go! Well there was this sergeant you see – can't remember his name – but he was a right nasty git, nobody liked him. It was his turn on the Sten, and there we was, three floors up. All the previous charges had weakened the floor, and when our charge went off the floor went with it."

He pauses to take breath. A cheeky smile stretches across his face.

Sword Beach, June 1944, looking inland.

"I suppose we could have stopped him going in, but I remember holding me mates back as he went in, Sten blazing. He was quite a sight as he disappeared; like a brick straight down a well. A couple of the lads outside saw him go – finger on the trigger all the way down. Broke a leg he did, and one of his arms. Proper result we thought."

We all laugh, sharing in the come-uppance of a nasty piece of work. "Still." The old soldier's smile slips slightly. "I suppose he had the last laugh. Whilst he was in hospital, we had D-Day, and we came in on the first day."

We all turn to face the beach – full of families enjoying the sun – and we imagine a very different day.

Sword Beach, June 2004.

Race you!

The coaches arrive at our destination. We are tired and hungry. We flow into the hotel. The proprietors are very happy to see us as they usher us in. Quickly the reception fills with people and suitcases – all trying to match up correctly. All around me happy faces are talking away to each other, all eager to get to the rooms for a quick wash and brush up before dinner. More crowd in: veterans, their families and friends, flow around me like a river, all trying to get to their rooms first. Suddenly I remember why I am there: I came on this trip of remembrance to help, and help I will. I spot one old veteran heading towards the crowded lift with suitcases in hand. He has not one, but two, hearing aids, and he is wearing an enamel badge telling all who can read that he is deaf, and could they kindly speak up. I intercept him, placing my hands on

Above: Old hat still fits.

his suitcases, attempting to grab them, and in a loud voice proclaim: "Here – let me help you."
His grip on his suitcases instantly tightens. I think at first that he has misheard me.
"I'll carry these for you." I say – still in a loud voice.
I glance at his room key, and notice he is on the third floor. "I will take them upstairs for you – you can take the lift." I smile encouragingly, hoping he heard me. The old veteran releases his vice-like grip on one suitcase, and I feel I am making progress. Then, with a wicked grin, he leans in close. His voice is low but easy to understand:
"Race you!" Then he is off.

Left to right:

Poppies wherever we go.

The Regimental Crest.

One of many resting places.

Good natured laughter fills the reception as everyone watches the scene, whilst I stand there open-mouthed. The old veteran is halfway up the first flight of stairs before I realise he is serious. I laugh out loud, grab the suitcase he left me, and set off in pursuit. The stairwell echoes to his laughter as we jostle for position on the second flight of stairs. I am much younger than he. I feel confident the race is won.

To this day I still cannot work out how I lost.

Royal Hotel, Caen centre, June 2004.

Two men

Two men stand looking over a field of corn ripening in the sun.   In the distance, obscured by a heat haze, Caen can be seen.

They do not know each other, these two men. They have just come to stand at a spot of land that means different things to each, but both are paying their respects.

Behind them stands the imposing concrete and steel fortification called 'Hillman'. On D-Day, 6th June 1944, the Royal Norfolk Regiment suffered heavily under it's guns - a nasty surprise for them, since no-one even realised it was there, they just stumbled upon it. Today, behind our two men, Hillman is not covered in gun smoke, nor do they hear the scream of shells flying overhead. There are no soldiers vying for control over the land. Today, Hillman is covered in flags, flapping lazily in the Summer breeze.

The screaming is of children scurrying to and fro as their families swarm over Hillman to remember. For today is the 6th June 2014.

One man turns to face the other. A hesitant conversation is started:

"Excuse me – you are English no? Did your relatives serve in the war?"

The second man turns to face the first, seeing a man not dissimilar in age and bearing to himself. He points to the sea of corn as he replies:

This page left:
Remembering old comrades at the Royal Norfolk Regiment Memorial, Norfolk House, Normandy.
Right:
Hillman fortification, June 2014.

"Yes – my father. He was a
Norfolk man. He was mortally
wounded in this field on D-Day
The first man casts his eyes away.
"I see." He says. He pauses, as if
unsure if he should continue. Then
he stands straighter, as if
shouldering a burden, holding
steady the second man's gaze.
"My father was the commanding
officer of the German garrison here
at Hillman on D-Day."
It is now the second man's turn to
hesitate. At the same time, both
hold out a hand. They shake in
greeting, nod to each other, then
turn back to face the field that
means so much to each, in
companionable silence.

Hillman, June 2014.

A COLLEVILLE-MONTGOMERY

Découvrez un Poste de Commandement
des Défenses Côtières, unique dans la région

LE SITE HILLMAN

Dans le Calvados, sur la Côte de Nacre
près de OUISTREHAM

Mémorial du Suffolk Regiment

The Suffolk Regiment Memorial

IN COLLEVILLE-MONTGOMERY

Take your time to explore a command post of
coastal defences. It's the only one in the region

HILLMAN SITE

In Calvados, on Côte de Nacre
near by OUISTREHAM

Top left:
The view out to sea from Hillman.

Middle and bottom left:
Veterans remember those who did not return.

Veterans and friends pay their respects at Norfolk House Memorial.

The Royal Norfolk Regiment

The NINTH OF FOOT

1685	Raised by King James II as Colonel Henry Cornwall's Regiment of Foot also known as the Ninth of Foot
1689/91	Ireland
1691/1703	Brest, the Mediterranean, Flanders
1704/07	Portugal and Spain
1708/62	Home service, Minorca, Gibraltar and Belle Isle
1762/76	Havana, Florida and home service
1776/88	American War of Independence, Canada, Saratoga
1782	Renamed the East Norfolk Regiment
1788/96	The West Indies
1797/1804	North Holland and Bremen
1799	The Badge of Britannia awarded to the Regiment
1804/08	Home service and Portugal
1808/09	Corunna and Walcheren
1809/13	The Peninsula, Gibraltar, Badajoz, Salamanca etc.
1813/27	Canada, the West Indies
1827/42	India – 1st Kabul campaign
1843/53	India – 1st Sikh War, England, Ireland, Malta
1853/56	The Crimean War
1856/81	The Ionian Islands, Japan, 2nd Afghan War
1881	Named 'The Norfolk Regiment'.
1881/99	Burma, India, South Africa
1899/1901	The South African War
1914/18	World War I – France, Mesopotamia, Dardanelles, Palestine
1919/39	Ireland, India, Mesopotamia, Aden, West Indies, Egypt, Shanghai
1935	King George V approved the distinction that the Regiment should, in future, be designated 'The Royal Norfolk Regiment'.
1939/45	World War II – France, Singapore, the Mediterranean, Northwest Europe, India, Burma, Malay
1951/59	Korea, Hong Kong, Cyprus, Germany
1959	With the Suffolk Regiment formed the 1st East Anglian Regiment
1967	With other East Anglian regiments formed the Royal Anglian Regiment of which 'A' Company, 1st Battalion, still carries forward the proud traditions of over 300 years of fine service.

The Regimental colours of The Royal Norfolk Regiment are yellow, red and black – the Regimental Colour carries the figure of Britannia on a yellow ground – red denotes infantry and black marks the part the Regiment played at the burial of Sir John Moore at Corunna in 1809.

Norfolk House: one of the Regiment's first objectives on D-Day, approximately one mile inland.

Above: A brief history of the Regiment.

Old and new

The notes of the 'Last Post' fade on the wind. We all fall quiet, heads bowed, the sun warm on our backs. The only sound is of the birds gently twittering in the fields, and even that seems muted, as if they can sense the mood. The 'Rouse' plays, filling the air with it's promise of something more than the end. Everyone starts to mingle.

The dedication of the new memorial has gone well. I look around at all who have attended. The French are there in great numbers; locals from the area, with a large dose of dignitaries. Interpreters are busy helping to breach the language barrier. The veterans – with their families and friends helping wherever they can – spend their time chatting to all, and each take a turn to stand by the memorial as the cameras click away.

Then I notice a group of very young men standing to one side. They wear suits, as do many of the people around us, yet they seem to hold themselves differently – a more proud bearing, as if ready at a moment's notice to take action if required. Then it occurs to me: they could be soldiers. As I walk towards them, I call out:

"Are you English?"

They all nod, and one calls back:

"Yes, we are."

I take a gamble:

"Which Regiment?"

Their spokesman smiles; a small, half-smile.

"We are all from the Royal Anglians. We heard the Royal Norfolks would be here today, so we came to pay our respects."

"Follow me." I say. "Our veterans will be thrilled to see you." Soon, old and young soldiers are chatting away. Decades separate them, yet they have all shared the same experiences of war. They are, after all, men who have been trained to do a very dangerous job. Governments and enemies change, but the job itself remains constant.

As I listen in, I hear tactics being discussed, and - more importantly - where to go for the best beer!

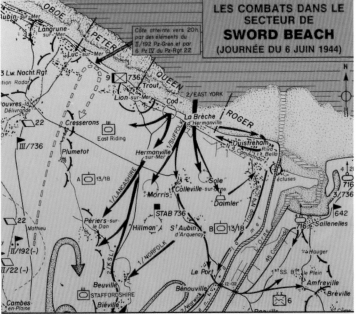

Two Officers of the 1st Battalion,
Royal Norfolk Regiment, 1945.

Veterans with their friends from Blainville,
France 2014.

Family and friends enjoy yet another fantastic meal
laid on by our hosts at Grimbosq, 2014.

Men of the Anti-Tank Platoon, 1944.

Memorial day

Above:
The Memorial on Sword Beach, Normandy.
It is so close to the beach, that behind it there is only sand and the sea.

The seagulls swirl and scream above us as we stand by the memorial. The day's sun has warmed it; the cold stone eagerly drawing in the heat. Now, it releases that heat on to our hands as we stoop to place our wreaths, laying them gently against the stone.

The local mayor speaks a few words as we stand respectfully. Behind me I hear the soft chink of cameras, mingling with the noise of traffic on the coast road. Then the ceremony is over and we wander, always keeping the memorial in sight, like an anchor for our emotions.

A man is introduced to me by the mayor; she tells me he is the artist who designed and sculpted the memorial. The mayor also tells us (in English far better than my French will ever be) that this man gave his time for the commission of the memorial free of charge. We all thank him for his fine work, and I ask him the significance of the woman looking down onto the soldiers as they struggle up the beach. He tells us of a woman, who, on D-Day, leant out of the window of her home on the edge of the beach, cheering the allies on and pointing out German positions.

"She was a brave woman to do this." I say.

He thanks me and explains:

"She was somewhat of a local legend, and also my mother."

I shake his hand and reply:

"She would be pleased to see what you have created here."

He smiles warmly at me, then states:

"She was very happy to see the allied soldiers on D-Day, as are we, to see the veterans return to remember the fallen. For here we never forget the blood spilled to make us free."

Above: Children of Blainville sit with the veterans during the service at their Memorial, June 2004.

Below: Memorial at Blainville, France.

Diary of campaign

1st Battalion THE ROYAL NORFOLK REGIMENT

D-Day 6th June 1944 to VE-Day 8th May 1945

1944 FRANCE		1945 HOLLAND	
6 June	Queen Red-Sword Beach, Rover	2 January	River Maas, Meerlo
7	Lebisey Wood		Blitterswilk, Hooge, Heide
	Norfolk House		Wijnhoverhof, Wanssum
	Blainville – Benouville	**BELGIUM**	
8 July	Lebisey Wood	8 February	Reken
11	Blainville	**GERMANY**	
	Ranville	25	Goch, (Pfalzdorf)
18	Manneville Wood	1 March	Kervenheim
25	Cazelle	2	Winnekendonk
3 August	Le Reculey	4	Haus Winkle
4	La Chapelle-aux-Huants	10	Till
5	La Bistiere	29	Rees
6	Pavee – Sourdevalle	2 April	Enschede
10	Le Reculey	4	Lingen
13	La Maslerie	8	Wallenhorst
17	Tinchebray	11	Barrien
3 September	Villers-en-Vexin	15	Brinkum
BELGIUM		21	Leeste
18	Soignies	25	Arsten
19	Peer	26	Bremen
HOLLAND		28	Delmenhorst
23	Asten	1 May	Bookholzburg
25	Helmond	5	Cease Fire 08-00hours
29	Bakel	8	VE-Day, Espelkamp
3 October	Heuman		
9	Cuijk		
11	St. Hubert, Haps		
12	Wanroij		
13	Overloon		
14	Attack to the Molen-Beek		
16	Over the Molen-Beek		
19	Heikant		
26	Venraij		
8 November	Oploo		
	Venraij		
24	Oostrum		
25	Wanssum		
3 December	Hape, St. Agatha, Oeffelt		
12	Germert		
16	East of Venraij - Ooijen		
	Wesserhof, Renkenshof		
	Eikelenbosch, Tienraij		
29	Horst		

Promise kept

We arrive at our destination: a quiet village in France. We stand outside an old barn that has been converted into someone's home. Children's toys lay scattered about the garden beneath a small brass plaque embedded into the wall of the old barn. You can just make out the words from the roadside. In front of the home, slightly to one side, stands a memorial. I help the veteran with us place a cross on it. We stand in silence as we watch the veteran pay his respects. There are three of us in this group. My friend turns to me and we shake hands, for today we have fulfilled a promise: after much research, we have helped the veteran standing before us locate this place, and make the trip to pay his respects. This is his first visit here. Many years have passed since the war's end, and it means a lot for him to be here.

After a while he turns to us and nods his head in gratitude, then we all head back to the car. As I help the veteran get comfortable in the back seat, I tell him jokingly to put his seat belt on, as we don't want to chance our luck. His head snaps round to me and his voice is strong and clear:

"Luck bor! Luck? I am the luckiest man alive! One of my best friends was killed standing by that barn. Machine gunned to death along with over a hundred of our soldiers, and the only reason I was not killed along with them, was luck. My friend and I were in a reinforcement company. Any unit needing replacements called on us for men. This officer came down the line. He needed seven replacements. My mate was seventh in line. I would have been number eight, but seven was wanted, so off he went. I never saw him again. If that officer had wanted eight men, there is a good chance I would be dead. If my mate had been standing on my left instead of my right, I'd be dead and you would be having this conversation with him. Luck bor! Sheer, blind, stupid luck!"

I glance back to the barn. The massacre at Le Paradis is a well known story. Nearly one hundred British soldiers were killed there; soldiers who had surrendered. I try to imagine myself standing against the barn wall - cold, tired and defenceless, then hearing the bolt being pulled back on a heavy machine gun, and, despite the warmth of the day, I shiver as I make my way to the driver's seat of the car.

Le Paradis War Cemetery.

This page;
Members of the Royal Norfolk Regiment Living
History Group pay their respects.

Below;
Meeting old and new friends in Holland, 2007.

Above: War damaged street in Holland, 1944.

Below: Villers-en-Vexin, France, 'S' Company Bren Gun Carriers.

Our good friends in Blainville, France.

Children of Blainville chatting to our veterans
in 2014.

Catch them stupid

The old soldier scoots down the road, walking stick beating a fast tattoo. I struggle to keep up. His voice drifts to me over his shoulder: "We spent a good couple of weeks here."

Around us, in the small French village, people go about their business. A steady flow of customers in and out of a baker's barely slows the old soldier as he skids around a corner. I catch up to him as he stands gazing over a parcel of land, closed in on three sides by old houses. The road narrows, forcing any traffic to slow as it negotiates the corner.

I struggle to regain my breath, a little embarrassed, since the old soldier is nearly twice my age, but he stands prouder than me, with no obvious signs of discomfort.

Perhaps he has been taken back to those years when he was young and strong, for his voice is clear, and his eyes bright as he speaks:

"They didn't know we had taken this village you see. Their convoys still kept coming through – four or five lorries at a time.

One of many ceremonies to honour our fallen.

We just sat on this corner, and they drove onto our guns. Lovely it was. We would clear the trucks out of the way, and wait for the next ones to come along, fat and dumb."
He turns to me, old face alive with the smile of a schoolboy.

You didn't often catch them being stupid, but when you did, it was great."
His voice turns wistful:
"Yes, we spent a good couple of weeks here."

Blainville, June 2006

Battalion HQ, Villers-en-Vexin, September 1944.

One more pancake

We are sitting around a large dining table in a lovely home. A wonderful smell of fresh, warm pancakes wafts through to us from the kitchen. To my right sits a veteran, happily munching on his second pancake provided by our hostess. His appetite is good and shows no sign of slowing down. To my left, another veteran flicks through photographs with our host. Their conversation is a mixture of pointing and lots of body language. One speaks no French, the other no English, yet it does not seem to diminish their obvious enjoyment.

Another round of pancakes wings it's way onto our plates, and the only sound for a few moments is the gentle clinking of cutlery and satisfied sighs. This is the first time I have visited our host's home. Our hostess - the pancake provider - speaks both French and English, and acts as interpreter on our journeys through Normandy. Each region has it's own mayors, and they all wish to welcome our veterans back to their soil each year. This lovely couple have helped our group in so

Above: Our very good friends.

many ways over the years, acting as go-betweens for our group and the many official parties in France. They always accompany us on the coach, sitting at the front, ready with directions, and they are always well organised with our itinerary. The thing I have noticed about them is that they are not just interpreters and organisers. They mean much more to us than that; they most definitely are

our friends.

Our hostess calls out as she leaves the kitchen: "Anyone want more?"
Most of us are more than full, and push our plates away, rubbing full tummies, yet the veteran to my right holds up his hand, and with a sticky grin replies:
"I'll have just one more pancake."

Normandy, 2004.

Humanity

"You went through ten partners whilst you were in France and Holland?"

The old veteran nods – his voice soft, almost tired, as he replies: "Yes – ten."

We sit overlooking a golf course. Behind us, inside the club house, the rest of our party finish yet another fabulous meal, organised by the Mayor of Blainville. I point down onto the golf course: "Look at him – if he keeps that up, he will be in England before us."

The veteran laughs with me as we watch a man swing ineffectively at his golf ball, lodged tight in a bunker, sand erupting like an explosion from each swipe. The veteran continues his tale; voice so low I struggle to hear.

"I think it was about the eigth partner I lost that made me realise I had seen too much – or was it the ninth? I can't even remember his face, but I remember very well how he copped it. I was the radio operator; two man job that, what with all the spare batteries and such like to lug about. We were prime targets. Kill us, and we lost contact with our support, so the Germans liked to pot us if they could.

Anyway, I was sitting in a foxhole, and my latest partner, a fresh replacement, sat with me. Then our position started to get mortared; nothing special, just a random bit of hate. Safest place to be is at the bottom of a nice deep foxhole, but the new lad, he kept sticking his head up to take a look. 'Sit down' I say, there's nothing to see! But he kept jumping up and down. Of course he got hit – straight in the neck. There he was, thrashing about in the bottom of the foxhole, blood pouring out of him. I'm trying to help, and keep the radio safe. The mortars are still falling, Then the medics show up, and they cart him off. Just like that.

Another partner gone, need a new replacement.

But what bothered me the most was not the fact that I had just seen another human being more than likely die in front of me. What bothered me the most, was that now I had to go on a long walk back to HQ, to get a new set of headphones, because he had bled all over them. Looking back, that was the moment it had all just become routine - the death and destruction I mean. That's when I started to lose my humanity.

When the war was over, my wife helped me to become human again; to laugh and be happy. A lot of blokes weren't that lucky though."

Above: Men of the Royal Norfolk Regiment in very different bunkers 1944/45.

We sit quietly together, and I try to
formulate an answer; to try and
make sense of it all. Then the
veteran nudges my arm and points
back to the bunker. The sand is still
flying. We both laugh out loud as a
golf club spins through the air.

Blainville golf club, 2004

Thanks must go to all our wonderful hosts, in all the countries we visit, for the warm welcomes, and all the lovely food and cake.
Once tasted, no one forgets the cake!

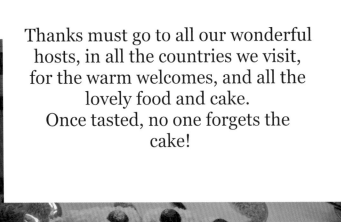

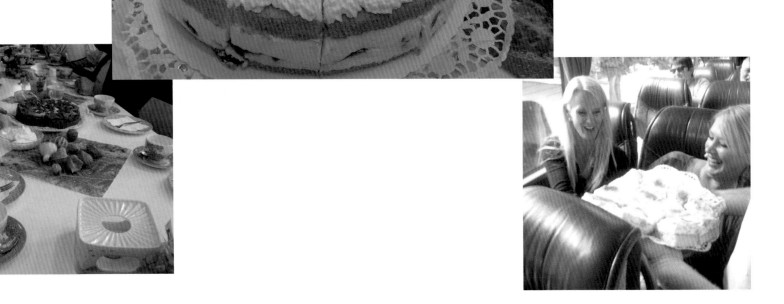

Not Enough Bullets!

As I stand on an old stone bridge across the River Orne, the water flows deep and wide beneath me. The old veteran standing with me looks at me, with eyes still strong despite the passing of the decades. His gaze takes in a farm about half a mile away, atop some high ground overlooking the River.

"You know." He says to me. "The first time I ever crossed this bridge, I was under fire."

I look around, trying to gauge the lie of the land, imagining all sorts of fire lines, where the Germans could have been positioned, shooting at him. He continued to speak as we both walked back towards the farm.

"As a despatch rider I had to ride all over, delivering orders and such like. Most of the time I was on my own. All I had for defence was a service pistol – six shots, short range – not a lot of cop really, so I wanted something better. I managed to snag me a Sten gun." Being a bit of a gun geek, I nodded in understanding.

"Still short-range." I said. "But a lot more bullets."

"Exactly." He replied. "So, there I was, riding along, Sten slung over my back, feeling pleased with myself. Then I rode around this corner, and disaster struck."

By now we had walked a fair way up the hill and I could see many places suitable for an ambush. Intrigued, I asked him:

"How many were shooting at you? Two? Three? Did you get to use your Sten gun?"

"Oh I used it alright, but there were no Germans – I was completely on my own." He stopped and pointed back down the road. "As I came round that corner, I hit an oil spill. My motorbike went one way, me the other, both of us bumping along the ground. The safety on a Sten gun is not too clever – it had a tendency to fire by itself if you dropped it hard enough - and me rolling along the ground at about twenty miles per hour classified as hard enough! Every time my back hit the ground, the damn thing went off! Each shot sounding like a thunder clap in my ear." He laughed out loud. "Looking back at it, it must have been a funny sight, but at the time I scared myself silly."

"Did you hurt yourself?"

"No – just a few scrapes and bruises. But I tell you - the first thing I did when I got back to HQ was to hand that Sten in and get my pistol back. I felt much safer with that by my side."

Above : The fateful bridge as it is today.

Below left: The River Orne, 2004.

Below right: Men in training, the despatch rider in the story is the one standing far right.

Football Match

The game is close: too close to call. The clock ticks down, and we all try our hardest to score the winning goal. It's England v France, in an impromptu friendly world cup, taking place on a patch of ground next to a farm near the River Orne. The French have fielded their youth team: a group of local children who arrived on their bicycles to meet our veterans. The English play their team of family and friends of the veterans, captained by one of those same veterans, sitting on the sideline with plenty of advice! The ball, well-loved, belongs to the farmer's young son. As soon as we all spotted it, laying lonely against the wall, nods were exchanged and jumpers were laid down (although on the English side suit jackets took the place of jumpers). What followed was a match few would forget.

The farm itself has seen many such battles play out in and around it's fields. We are here to remember the fallen of the 7th Battalion, who fought a much more vicious encounter than ours. They courageously held a bridgehead across the River Orne, near this farm. The Germans tried very hard to throw them back over the river, but the Norfolks stubbornly refused to give in.

At the bottom of the farm drive sits a memorial, remembering those who lost their lives. The family who own the land welcome back the veterans of that conflict with open arms and much generosity of spirit whenever they can visit. We all pay our respects to a much darker time in their history, and pour light over it with good food and good company.

The result of the football match: England: 5, France: 6. Needless to say, our captain was unimpressed.

Brunel's farm yard, 2004.

The Brunel's farm near the River Orne, France.

Ready for night patrol into no mans land, 1944/45.

Cooking in the field; never an easy task!

Never too old for a belly rub!

Right place, right time

Proud veterans surround me, shaking my hand, patting me on the back. Many are the calls of 'well done' and 'thank you'. My throat locks up. Their faces blur before my eyes. I have just finished playing the Last Post for a group of British Commandos in Normandy. I know none of the men before me, I just happened to be in this particular cemetery to play for another party. The standard bearer for the Commandos had spotted me and asked:

"Can you play that old bugle or is it just for show?"

So, I played for a group of men who undoubtedly were some of the first to storm fortress Normandy in 1944, to help them pay their respects to their fallen comrades. Now, with them still thanking me, my eyes cast over the faces of these old Commandos.

The different cap badges of so many Regiments pass before me, all united under the Commando badge. One old man clasps my hand between both of his.

"Thank you young man, thank you very much. You don't know how much it means to us that you were here."

No words can describe how I feel. I have served my country in peace time, but all of these men before me have served their country in a time of cold, hard, brutal war, *yet they are thanking me for what I have just done.* Barely trusting myself to speak, I shake his hand and say:

"No. Thank *you*, thank you all."

Above: Ceremony at Pavée France.

Above: Veterans and widows gather at the Pavée
memorial.

During World War Two the Royal Norfolk
Regiment won five Victoria Crosses. The most for
any Regiment during the war.
Corporal Sidney Bates won his on this ground.
Sadly he died of wounds received.

Above:
Old comrades meeting for the first time
since the end of WW2.

This bor's a boyo!

"You're Welsh – why were you in the Norfolk Regiment?"

My question was received with a grin and a twinkle of the eye.

"I was asked almost that exact same question many years ago, almost on this exact same spot. As to why I was in the Norfolks – that's a story for a different time, but I will give you the same answer I gave the man who asked me back then if you are interested."

The dapper veteran stands with me overlooking a small valley. On the high ground, on which we stand, a fierce battle took place. The Germans threw in a counter attack here, trying to push the allies back. They met fierce resistance from a mixed group of the Monmouthshire Regiment and the Royal Norfolks, who - as fate would have it - were in the process of relieving the Monmouthshires. The veteran looks around, getting his bearings.

"Just over there it was. The Norfolks

Above : The local school came and sung to us, 2014.

were tasked with relieving the Monmouthshires – a famous Welsh Regiment. There was only one road in and out of this high ground, so we were doing it by companies – one in, one out. I was point man, one of the first Norfolks to arrive up here. We were hailed by them as we approached:

"Halt – who goes there?"

"The Royal Norfolks."   Says I.

"The Royal Norfolks?" Says he. "The Royal Norfolks? You're Welsh boyo – what are you doing with them?"

The veteran pauses, looks me in the eye, and, with a face full of humour, continues:

"Welsh? Aye – that I am boyo. But I'm a mercenary an' I".

Pavée, June 2004.

A good idea at the time

"So - this is your hill?"

My question was met with an embarrassed snort of amusement. The old soldier standing with me looked along the road as it wound it's way down into a valley. He took out his tobacco pouch, and pointed down to a village nestling at the bottom.

"See that church down there?"

I could just make out a steepled roof below us in the distance. As I nodded in reply, out of the corner of my eye I noticed the rest of our coach party clustered around a road sign on the corner of the road. My attention snapped back to the veteran as he continued his story between puffs on his roll up.

"We were told to reinforce a unit on the other side of that village. Our convoy started out early morning, using the mist for cover. We got about a third of the way down when the sun burnt off the mist and we stood out like a pimple on a baby's bum. The Germans spotted us, and opened up on the convoy with their 88's from across the valley. Luckily they were after the vehicles and were using armour-piercing rounds, not high explosives. As the shells came in there were three of us on foot in front of the convoy as vanguard. Our vehicles popped smoke and pulled back. Unfortunately that left me and my mates hunkered down, swinging in the wind, with the Germans still firing their 88's into the smoke. So I thought 'sod this' and I started to run. It was too far to go back with the vehicles and besides, most of the fire was going towards them, so I ran downhill. My two mates soon joined me. As we ran, I swear I could see the rounds skipping off the road in front of us and slamming into the bank. We ran all the way down this road in our size 10 boots, under fire. As we reached the church wall, we were going too fast to stop, so we all just bundled over it, and we lay there in a heap in the middle of the graveyard – all arms and legs, panting away. In a right state we were. Then a sergeant of the unit we were to reinforce came around the corner. 'Who are you lot?' he asked. I looked up at him from the ground and said:

'We're your reinforcements sergeant.' He looked at us laying there, shook his head and said: 'Gawd 'elp us'. Then disappeared back around the corner. The three of us looked at each other and just started to laugh."

I looked at the old soldier.

"So you ran all the way down this hill and into that village, under fire the whole time?"

He grinned at me whilst creating his own smoke screen.

"Seemed like a good idea at the time." Fag break over, we headed back to the coach. As we passed the road sign I noticed someone had scribbled in one corner. I stepped over to it and grinned as I made out the inscription:

'Fred's Hill.'

Pavée on Perrier ridge, June 2004.

Right: The view down into the valley where the church can be clearly seen.

Bottom Right: My good friend standing on 'his' hill.

Below: Shell damage to an orchard in France.

Smile for.....

.....the camera.

Above: Memorial at Kervenheim, 2008.

Above: Cake at Kervenheim, September 2014.

Above: Officers planning group in the field, France 1944.

Fraud?

The sun broke through the cloud cover as we finished our first visit to one of many cemeteries on our itinerary for the day. It is a sombre experience, walking amongst the dead; rows of stone laid out in neat, straight lines. Today, the early morning air smells fresh and crisp, with the scent of newly mown grass. Our group of veterans, their families and friends, wander amongst the headstones, lost in quiet moments of contemplation. One veteran comes to stand by my side, leaving his family to walk the field of graves. I have the greatest respect for our veterans, for what their generation had to endure. He turns to me and speaks:

"You know - I feel such a fraud." His words shock me, and I remain quiet as he continues:

"I spent my war repairing boots. Everyone looks at me as if I was some kind of hero. The closest I got to any danger in Europe was when German planes strafed our convoy a few times. These men laying here in cemeteries are the real fighting men. I lived. Many better men than me died. Why did I deserve to survive?"

He stood, head bowed, worry and self-doubt etched across his face. My mind raced, looking for answers. I could not think of anything to say that would help, so I just started to talk:

"You come back each year to pay your respects to these men. You bring your family with you as well. You feel that you did not fight, but you are fighting now to keep their memory alive. You have lived a life denied so many, and lived it well. You can do no more to honour them."

He gave no reaction to my words. He only sighed and moved off to where his family stood. He smiled for them as they all gestured around the headstone of a Norfolk soldier. Later that same day, at another cemetery, the clergyman holding the service gave a sermon on forgiveness. He explained that, after sixty years of peace, it was time to forgive and move on. Not just to forgive ones enemies, but to forgive oneself for surviving. His words struck me, and I glanced to where my friend stood with his head bowed. I hoped he had found his answers.

Overloon War Cemetery, 2006.

Above: Men of the Regiment moving though the ruins of a town.

Flowers

As we sit drinking coffee on the pavement, we enjoy the hustle and bustle of the High Street going past us. The cafe we have chosen is busy, vibrant with life. Six of us are chatting happily. One of us is a veteran in his wheelchair, medals shining in the sun, beret set just-so on his head. His hands are the largest and strongest I have ever seen. He uses them well to cradle his coffee, savouring every sip. A quiet strength flows from him. We eagerly listen as he tells us of long ago - when he travelled through here for the first time, sat upon a very different set of wheels – of the smoke, of the devastation. He tells us how happy the people were to see them as the Germans retreated. The crowds flowing out onto the rubble-strewn streets to welcome them.

He pauses to sip at his coffee. We sit back and wonder how it must have felt. Then, suddenly, from the passing crowd, a woman appears. She is holding a bouquet of the most beautiful flowers. She thrusts

Above: One of many to whom we owe a great debt in 2005, and with his fellow recruits in 1936.

them into the hands of our veteran, and speaks a few soft words as she kisses him lightly on his cheek. "For our liberators – thank you." Then – as quickly as she appeared – she is gone, the crowd swallowing her up. We are in shock, unsure of what has just happened in front of our eyes. Our veteran sits, head held high, eyes open wide, but he is many years away.

His large, strong hands gently grasp the flowers. His coffee sits forgotten, half spilled on to the table. Then his tears start to flow, and we wonder no more.

Helmond Market Place, September 2005

Chocolate

Above: Our Veterans giving out chocolate to the children of Venray, 2014.
Behind them to the right is a man who remembers vividly being a child in Arnhem, and British troops of the Polar Bear Division giving him chocolate.

Below: Entertainment laid on for us in Venray.

As the allies slowly liberated Europe, they discovered many stories of hardships suffered by civilians during the occupation of their countries. Holland in particular suffered a shortage of food, and many British soldiers found themselves surrounded by children, clamouring for whatever they could get. Chocolate was always a firm favourite if it could be scrounged. One such child used to follow the Royal Norfolk soldiers around as they wandered the streets of Helmond. He became a regular sight amongst the troops. So much so, that on the day they pulled out, he followed them on his pushbike. But of course the lorries were too fast for him and he was soon left behind. The troops in the trucks shouted words of encouragement to him as they threw chocolate bars over the side for him to pick up.

Every year, as the veterans return to visit the countries they helped liberate, they still like to give chocolate bars to the schools, and to any children introduced to them. It has become a tradition both sides look forward to. On one particular visit to Helmond a man wandered up to the veterans and handed them an envelope. Inside was a large cheque made out to the Royal Norfolk Regiment Association, plus a simple note. It read: '*Enclosed cheque for chocolate bars, plus many years interest. Thank you, from the boy on the bike.*'

Every year at Venray War Cemetery, each headstone has a rose placed in remembrance, by the Scout group of Venray. It is a moving ceremony to watch. As the young children move among the headstones to lay their flowers, a splash of colour is left on the graves, forging a link from the past to the future.

Right:
Proud standard bearer,
Venray War Cemetery,
Holland 2014.

Clockwise from top left : Officers of the Regiment in the field 1944, Helmond High Street, Helmond Market Place, Helmond High Street.

People ask: 'Why do we go back each year?' 'Why go back to the same places each time?'
In reply there is no one answer.

"We go to pay our respects."

" I go for the camaraderie of the group."

"I go back to see the ground my father fought on ."

"I go to keep faith with my old comrades."

"We go so my family can see why my father died."

"I go for the friendship and the cake!"

"I go to see my friends in Europe."

"I go to face my nightmares."

"I go to visit my husband's grave."

"We go because they can't come home."

Above: Royal Norfolk Regiment 'D' Company, May 1945

Below: Arnhem Memorial.

Below: Our veterans giving a talk to a classroom of Dutch children in Arnhem, Holland, 2004.

Above:
Royal Norfolk Plain, Helmond:- a small square, part of Helmond City dedicated to the Royal Norfolk Regiment, enclosed by nine oak trees, which represent the Ninth Regiment of Foot.

Alone amongst strangers

Molen Beek September 2014.

"I remember one young lad very well, although I never really got to see his face properly."
We are all standing on a large open area of ground, split by a small river - what the Dutch call a 'Beek'.
"He joined us the night before we attacked over the Molen Beek. He reported to me as a replacement whilst it was still dark, and I assigned him to a platoon."
The wind blows hard across the field, causing our veteran to stagger slightly. A few of us move forward to help, but it is not necessary – he has already steadied himself.
"That same night we had to lay in this field ready for a dawn attack across the Beek. Our target was that village over there."
As he talks, the years flow away, and we are lying with him in that field – cold, and unsure of our chances for survival.

"Near dawn, our artillery started it's preliminary bombardment to cover us. Unfortunately one of the guns was firing short – it was landing right in amongst us. We all hugged the ground hard. I can still remember the smell of the grass and the soil, strong in my nose. Finally, after what seemed like hours, the time to attack came, and our artillery stopped. We rose to our feet, but sadly a lot of us never got up. As I ran past one man – lying face down – I tried to get him moving, but he was one of the dead. I realised then – it was the replacement."

Our veteran bows his head, the sadness in his face easy to hear in his voice.

"We all had a very hard job to do, fighting this war, but most of us fought amongst friends. I felt so very sad for that boy. He joined us, laid down, and died amongst strangers."

He stops talking, still gazing out over the Beek. We all remain quiet. Even the wind drops.

Molen Beek, September 2014.

Above :
'S' Company officers, September 1944.

Right: Molen Beek Memorial, 1988.

Left: Walking the Beek one more time, September 2014.

DEDICATED
TO THE MEN OF
THE 1ST BATTALION
THE ROYAL NORFOLK REGIMENT
WHO SUFFERED AND DIED
IN THE FIELDS AROUND
THIS VERY PLACE IN OCTOBER 1944

MAY PEACE AND FREEDOM
BE THEIR LIVING MEMORIAL

THIS MONUMENT WAS RAISED
BY THEIR COMRADES AND FRIENDS
FROM BRITAIN AND THE NETHERLANDS

Molen Beek Memorial.

Luck

Above: Collecting German prisoners in a newly liberated town, 1944.

As the two of us sit and chat, I learn the true meaning of luck. The old man in front of me talks slowly, as if every word pulls him back in time:

"We were tasked with a patrol. Six of us sent out just to keep an eye on the land, make sure no-one is sneaking up on us, you know the sort of thing."

He waves his hand at me, pulling me in closer. "None of us was a rookie – we all knew what we were doing. Anyway, we were moving along, keeping quiet, when a machine gun opened up. Just harassing fire, not aimed at us, but it came close - too close for comfort.

We all hit the dirt as quick as we could. All of us except one lad. His webbing got caught on some wire in the hedgerow, and before any of us could help, the next burst of fire stitched right across him."

He pauses, eyes wide, staring into the past. "You know – even in death he didn't fall to the ground, just hung there like a scarecrow.

It just goes to show you that all the training and experience in the world can't save you, if luck isn't with you."

I hate getting wet

The rain fell. It puddled under our feet, creating patterns in the soil, as we made our way to the river bank. Barges full of cargo sedately wound their way down river, heading towards the call of the sea.

I hold an umbrella over my friend as he stands staring across the river. I look behind us with a wistful gaze at the warm cafe we left to come and stand here. The rain falls in a steady pitter patter of sound on the tight fabric as I listen to my friend: "We spent some of the winter of '44 here. The snow was up to our knees – coldest winter in recorded memory it was."

I shiver as some of the rain falls down my neck, and I jostle for a bit more space under the umbrella. My friend – a veteran of WW2 – laughs at my discomfort.

"You." He says with a really big grin on his face "Would not have liked the cold!" I nod my head in

Above: War torn street, Holland.

agreement. "But surely you had billets – somewhere to keep warm?" I asked. He smiles at me. "Yes we had billets – in a small village near here called Blitterswijk. None of us could pronounce it properly and the Germans used to stonk it regularly just to keep us honest. So we all called it 'Blitz me quick'!" We

both laugh at the joke, then I grimace as more rain finds it's way down my back. My friend laughs even harder, then takes pity on me and we walk back to the warm cafe.

Near the River Maas, September 2005.

Above and right: Winter of 1944, Blitterswijk.

Below: Helmond.

Memorial at Kervenheim.

Kervenhiem 2014.

High price to pay

We walk along a trail fitting snugly between the woods on our right, and a field on our left. We have left the rest of our party behind, finishing their picnic in a small clearing.
The day is warm – not a cloud in the sky. Across the field the small village of Kervenheim can be seen. Around us the birds sing their songs, and the voices of our friends carry to us on the wind.

The veteran with me is silent - listening to sounds long remembered in his head, of different friends chatting. The gravel crunches under our feet as we walk. Then he stops and points off the trail into the woods.
"Time plays with terrain and memory, but it was around about here that we all stopped for a cigarette and a chat."
I retrieve a small cross from my

pocket, and place it at the base of the nearest tree. We stand together in silence; one remembering, one wondering. Then, with a sigh, the veteran turns to face the ploughed field. His voice is sad as he speaks:
" Of course, that for many of them was their last cigarette. We advanced to take Kervenheim across this field.

The noise was terrible – machine guns,
mortars and our own artillery adding to
the din..."
He pauses, again remembering.
"By the end of the day we had taken
the place. But what a price we paid.
There were not many of us left
standing".

I look back into the woods and imagine
the young soldiers sitting chatting to
one another about home and their
loved ones. My eyes fall to the cross,
and I hope someone, some day, will
see it, and wonder why it is there. The
veteran – once one of the young
soldiers – lays his hand on my
shoulder.
"Come on – let's get back to the rest of
them – our walk's done."
Around us the birds sing on...

Kervenheim, 2014.

Above and below: Kervenheim, September 2014.

Above: The children of Blitterswijk catch our veterans for a chat in 2008.

Above: We will remember them.

Above: This man is Dutch. He joined the Regiment as an interpreter, and served with distinction through to the end of the war. After the war he returned to being a teacher.

Left: Ranks upon ranks of stone.

Above: Remembering fallen friends.

Left: British troops in a newly
liberated German town.

This page: Kervenheim, 2004.

Kervenheim,
1945 and 2014.

Flip side

I march once again with my old comrades in arms. Our heads are held high, shoulders back. The gravel crunches beneath our feet, and old rhythms come back to mind. Our arms swing, and I am not the only one humming marching tunes under my breath. As we round the corner, our target comes into sight. The war memorial is clean, as it should be. The white stone stands out starkly in the sun.

Clustered around it are a small group of men as old as us. In younger days we fought over this ground battling to the death. We lost many friends here and so did they. Now we all come together to pay our respects to those we remember. No more hatred fills our hearts, only sorrow for our lost comrades, tinged with hope for a better future.

Their service of remembrance is complete, and one of our number who speaks their language well, asks them to join us at the civilian memorial. Many civilians died here – ordinary men and women who did not, or could not, leave their homes in times of war. Our old enemies readily agree. They have brought a bugler with them; we ask him to play for us. The local priest conducts the service. There is no blame laid at anyone's feet, for war is a vile and hateful thing. We all had jobs to do, and we all fought hard for our friends.

The service concludes with the bugle's notes floating away on the wind. We all shake hands – old comrades and old enemies - all together. I seek out the bugler to thank him, for he played well. The young bugler is talking with the veterans he has accompanied to this spot. I know not his language, so I speak to him in mine, as I shake his hand:

"Wunderbar brass, mein Freund, wunderbar brass."

Kervenheim, 2004.

War damaged streets.

Above: Kervenheim civilian memorial, 2004.
Below: Kervenheim, 1945.

These two pages: Men of the Regiment working and living in the field, France, Holland & Germany, 1944/1945.

The sound of the shells

"When you've been doing this job for a long time, you get to know the sounds of the shells; what fired them, where they're going. Anyway – we heard this lot going off and I said: 'They're meant for us.' So we legged it, trying to get into some slit trenches. Everyone made it except me. The last shell landed, picked me up like a rag doll and slammed me down hard. Got peppered with shrapnel, and that was the end of my war. After nearly five years fighting I celebrated VE Day from a hospital bed in Stoke on Trent."

Veteran's Return

We gaze across the busy beach, yet I sense he sees: a different scene entirely to the one in front of me.
Bodies lay where children play. Noise, confusion, terror, take their toll.
Am I worthy to look into his eyes, whilst they bare so much of his soul?

The road down which we travel next - an easy drive today - he trudged step by weary step; numb from fighting, features grey.
A distant tree line - no different to any others I can see - is scrutinised with grateful thanks; it was his sanctuary.
Too many others tried, yet failed, to make it to that place. Lads who were like brothers, ran the ultimate race.

We pull over by a field – one of many: flat and plain. His hand comes up, and presses lightly on the window pane.
A fierce and bloody battle superimposed in his head. Comrades fighting by his side, then suddenly they're dead.
As we re-trace this old man's steps, he recounts trials of bloody fights. He's paid for his survival with many years of sleepless nights.

We pay our respects to rows of his pals, whose stories remain untold. He pictures their fresh young faces, denied the chance to grow old.
And he wonders again (for the umpteenth time): 'Why him? Why not me?
That boy was no worse a soldier, had no less desire to be free.'

As these old veterans join the ranks of those who've gone before, and their tales are filed away under the sterile heading 'War',
Become a 'Memory Guardian': an honourable friend. Someone who can state with faith:

"We Will Remember Them."

Acknowledgements:
Many thanks are due to all who have contributed to this book. Those who have supplied photos, told their stories, been there for the group, and been there for us.

Grateful thanks also to our generous sponsors, for their faith in this project.

Further reading about the 1st Battalion Royal Norfolk Regiment can be found in the following book: "Thank God and the Infantry" by John Lincoln. This book recalls the experiences of the foot soldiers at the front, told in their own words, from D-Day to VE-Day. It is the life of the poor bloody infantry.